Abou

Audrey Farley (nee Ware) was born in Reading, Berkshire. After spending many holidays in Sussex during the 70's and 80's she moved in 1987 with her husband Alan to Telscombe Cliffs. It was their belief that their then young children would have a better quality of life in Sussex. They have never regretted the move.

In 1992 she went to an adult education class in Hove on "Tracing your family tree" run by Pam Simons. The genealogy bug bit hard and has never let go. She feels her biggest success in genealogy was, with the help of friends, uniting her niece Simone with her father whom she had never met, even though at the outset of the search his surname was unknown!

She spends a lot of her time walking in and around Telscombe Village with her Border Collie "Shadow" and loves the downs. It is her wish to be buried in Telscombe Churchyard, one of the most tranquil places on earth.

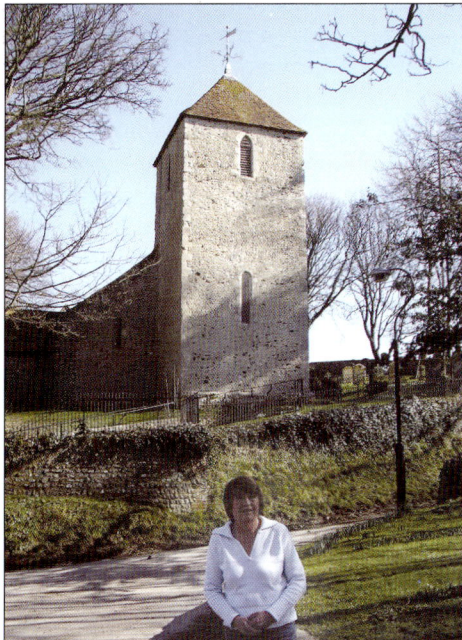

I dedicate this book to my family.
Alan, my husband, Andrew my son and Michelle, my daughter.

They have put up with my obsession for genealogy
very patiently for the past 15 years.

I would like to acknowledge the following for their help in compiling this book. Malcolm Troak, whose past experience and collection of old Telscombe postcards has proved invaluable. Barry N.Cornes for using Telscombe Parish for his thesis entitled "Telscombe c1780-c1871". Peter Higginbotham, for allowing me to use material from his excellent website located at www.users.ox.ac.uk/~peter/workhouse. Jacqueline Pollard, whose connections in the Australian genealogical world helped me greatly. Pam Simons and the Micawber Club, who between them taught me everything I know about family and local history and the present incumbent of Telscombe parish, The Revd. D.A. Hider, for passing on the village "folklore" to me. To all, many thanks.

Introduction

Telscombe is a beautiful unspoilt village in Sussex tucked in a hollow in the South Downs. It is at the end of an unclassified road and has no through traffic. It has neither a pub, nor a shop nor a school. Hill walkers frequent the village, often using the youth hostel there but other than that, Telscombe has remained largely unchanged for centuries. It is mentioned in the Doomsday Book but it dates back well before that and still has a fine Saxon Tower.

The Saxon Tower at Telscombe

In 1821 the population was 113. By 1851 Telscombe's population had risen to 176, with 35 households (12 of these households, 67 people in all, were Coastguards and their families). By 1991 the population had risen to 6,504, with 2,932 households but this by now encompassed the 20th century built Telscombe Cliffs, from which the village is still detached. The village has very little claim to fame. There have been connections with smuggling in centuries past and nearby the original 16th Century Coastguard cottages are still there in Telscombe Cliffs, although they have now been converted into a public house/restaurant. In 1902 a Grand National winner, *Shannon Lass* owned by the village Squire and benefactor Ambrose Gorham, was trained on the gallops at Telscombe. There is a memorial to Gracie Fields in the churchyard on the tombstone of her brother Tom Stansfield.

The Coastguard Station, Telscombe Circa 1912

But in a very old Telscombe Town Guide Book I read one other thing that puts Telscombe well and truly on the historical map:

"An interesting record in the Burial Register shows the name of James Lulham, Telscombe, buried 1st September 1819, aged 39 years. He was the last man to be hanged in England for sheep-stealing."

This intrigued me and I wondered if he really was and if it could be proved or disproved. I immediately went on the Internet to see what I could find.

I soon found out he was not the last. At least two others, Thomas Fairhead and William Gillot, were hanged at Chelmsford in 1820 for sheep stealing. There were probably many others who were hanged for this crime after that date, as capital punishment for this offence was still on the statute a decade later. Many attempts to repeal capital punishment were made. In 1823 and 1830, Robert Peel, the Home Secretary, obtained legislation that removed the death penalty from over one hundred crimes. It was not until 1832 that "horse and sheep-stealing and coining" ceased to be hanging offences.

	1800-1834	1835-1864	1865-1899
Sentenced to Death	29808	3014	898
Hanged for Murder	523	336	485
For other crimes	2153	27	0
Total hanged	2676	363	485
Reprieved	27132	2651	413

I decided that I would like to find out more about James Lulham, our local infamous citizen, so I started by looking in the East Sussex County Record Office, The Maltings, Castle Precincts, Lewes to see what I could uncover.

The original entry, in the burial register for the church of St Laurence Telscombe, is entered as normal but there is a note in the margin written in a different hand than that of the vicars which says "The last man hanged for sheep stealing?" It seemed to be a question asked by an observer rather than a fact and there is no mention of England at all. This visit and what I discovered led me on to the Local Studies Library in Church Street, Brighton, The National Newspaper Library, at Colindale, London, The National Archives at Kew, Horsham Museum, Horsham Library, Newhaven Museum and The West Sussex County Record Office at Chichester. As well as this, it gave me the excuse to visit some of the prettiest villages in Sussex. So, starting at James' birth village of Falmer, the story takes us on to Telscombe, Rottingdean, Horsham Common, Botany Bay and the tiny village of Botolphs and ends in Telscombe's neighbouring parish of Newhaven.

The burial entry in Telscombe's church records

(Ref. PAR 491/1/5/1)

So this then is the story of James Lulham of Telscombe and a few other
characters encountered on the way.

Chapter One
James' Origins

James Lulham was born on August 9th 1780 in Falmer, Sussex, the 5th son of John and Elizabeth Lulham. There may have been two different Elizabeth's, wife of John as the burial and marriage registers for Falmer, respectively show an Elizabeth Lulham buried there on February 10th 1774 and a marriage between a John Lulham and Elizabeth Harris (both of this parish) on April 9th 1776. James was one of ten known children to be born to this couple. I would think that the family were fairly middle class although this is only a presumption as they had been educated sufficiently to be able to write. There was a charity school in Falmer at this time. Anthony Spingett (1652-1735) left by will an Exchequer annuity of £10 per annum, which ran until 1806 to Falmer School. Falmer had 26 families in 1724 and a population of 255 in 1801.

St Laurence Church Falmer

Another reason for presuming that they were possibly middle class is the fact that James' elder brother John married a schoolmaster's daughter, Charlotte Waters, in the then adjacent parish of Rottingdean on October 18th 1798. Charlotte's father, John Waters (1746-1820), is listed in a book entitled "Sussex Schools of the 18th Century" by John Caffyn. There it describes him as a schoolmaster and vestry clerk of Waldron, who was also the Governor of the Workhouse. It seems unlikely that a man in his position would allow his daughter to be married to a mere agricultural labourer.

St Margaret's Church, Rottingdean

James, however, did not *apparently* seem to make such a good match. On October 31st 1804 he married Elizabeth Hobden of Telscombe at St Laurence Church in Telscombe. He signed his name but Elizabeth made her mark with an X. Their first known child, Mary Ann, was baptised at Rottingdean, also then adjacent to the parish of Telscombe, on April 13th 1806. By 1809 James and Elizabeth were back in Telscombe where their daughter Harriot was baptised on April 3rd. Another daughter, Elizabeth was baptised at Telscombe on April 3rd 1813. This time James' occupation was given as "shepherd". So he had a fairly poor occupation by the standards of the day.

References from the East Sussex Record Office.

Rottingdean Baptisms	1783-1812	Par 466/1/1/4
Rottingdean Marriages	1754-1812	Par 466/1/1/3
Falmer Baptisms	1740-1803	Par 327/1/1/2
Falmer Marriages	1740-1803	Par 327/1/1/4
Falmer Burials	1740-1802	Par 327/1/1/2
Telscombe Baptisms	1775-1812	Par 491/1/1/2
Telscombe Baptisms	1813-1954	Par 491/1/2/1
Telscombe Marriages	1757-1810	Par 491/1/1/3
Telscombe Burials	1775-1812	Par 491/1/1/2
Telscombe Burials	1813-1983	Par 491/1/5/1

The dew pond on the Tye at Telscombe, circa 1930's.
Shepherds took their sheep to water here.
It has recently been restored.

St Laurence Church, Telscombe, circa 1943.

John Lulham = Elizabeth ?

Thomas Lulham	Benjamin Lulham	Ann Lulham	Francis Lulham	Fanny Lulham	John Lulham	James Lulham	Mary Ann Lulham	Jenny Lulham	Isaac Lulham
Baptised 19th Oct 1766	Baptised 29th Jan 1769	Baptised 7th Apr 1771	Baptised 11th July 1773	Baptised 29th Dec 1776	Baptised 6th Dec 1778	Born 9th Aug 1780 Baptised 10th Sept 1780	Baptised 7th July 1782	Baptised 7th June 1784	Baptised 28th May 1786
Falmer Sussex	Falmer Sussex	Falmer Sussex	Falmer Sussex	Falmer Sussex	Falmer Sussex	Falmer Sussex	Falmer Sussex	Falmer Sussex	Falmer Sussex

The known children of John and Elizabeth Lulham who were all baptised in St Laurence's Church, Falmer. In the baptism records James' birth date was also given.

Chapter Two
James' Fortunes Improve

On July 7th 1816 James and Elizabeth had a daughter, Louisa, privately baptised. This was usually done if the infant's life was in danger. Happily Louisa survived long enough to be fully received into Telscombe Church on November 24th 1816. This time however, James' occupation is given as yeoman. A yeoman was a land owning farmer of some standing. How could James have risen from a shepherd to this? The records of Telscombe Manor revealed all.

James' wife Elizabeth (nee Hobden) inherited copyhold land in Telscombe from her uncle Samuel. The Manor records, dated July 9th 1812 record that; -

"9 July 1812
Also at this court the homage present that Samuel Hobden who held of the lord of the manor to him and his heirs by coop of court roll at the will of the lord accordingly to the custom of the said manor all that customary messuage one barn one garden and out yard and one half of land with the appurtenaures thereto belonging and adjoining situate lying and being in Telscombe in the county of Sussex paying to the lord yearly fffifteen shillings and sixpence....................
..... to the lord for an heriot one ewe sheep compounded for the sum of eighteen shillings...............
......Elizabeth the wife of James Lulham of Southwick on the county of Sussex shepherd late Elizabeth Hobden spinster which said Elizabeth was the only child of Thomas Hobden deceased who was the younger brother that left any issue of the said Samuel Hobden and as such his heir and according to the custom of the said manor his heir and entitled to the said messuage lands tenements and premises (save as aforesaid) and desired to be admitted to the said messuage lands tenements and premises as aforesaid as her right and inheritance according to the custom of the said manor."

Ref. East Sussex Record Office AMS 6104 (Court Book) fol. 13

Richard Hobden = Ann

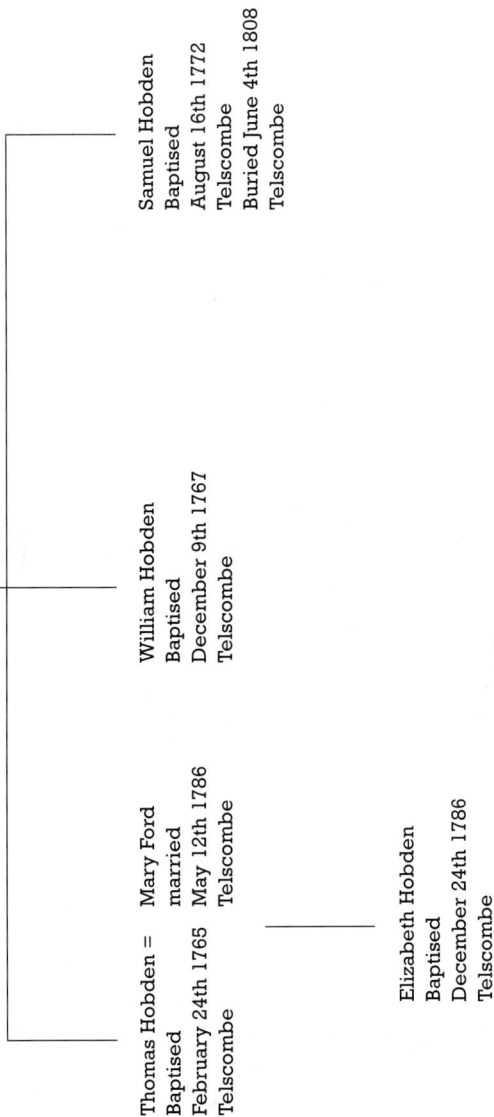

Thomas Hobden =
Baptised
February 24th 1765
Telscombe

Mary Ford
married
May 12th 1786
Telscombe

William Hobden
Baptised
December 9th 1767
Telscombe

Samuel Hobden
Baptised
August 16th 1772
Telscombe
Buried June 4th 1808
Telscombe

Elizabeth Hobden
Baptised
December 24th 1786
Telscombe

*The Manor House in Telscombe Village
where the Court may have sat.*

James and Elizabeth had inherited a substantial quantity of land in Telscombe. The 1811 Enclosure map of Telscombe shows that they owned 20 separate strips of land, totalling 13 acres and 3 roods, making them the 4th largest landowners (copyholders) in the parish. Things were looking up. The reference in the manor record of *"James Lulham of Southwick"* led me to look at the Southwick baptism registers (West Sussex Record Office, Chichester) to see if any children of this couple were baptised there. I only found one entry, A Harriet Lulham, daughter of James and Elizabeth was baptised there on December 31st 1809. The Telscombe couple had already had a daughter called Harriot baptised at Telscombe on April 3rd same year. Maybe she was baptised twice, once in each parish.

St Michael and All Angels Church, Southwick

1818 arrived and it was to be the beginning of a downturn in fortunes in the Lulham's household. It started off very sadly. On January 25th 1818 James and Elizabeth buried the same daughter, Harriot, in Telscombe. She was 8 years old. How or why she died we will never know. They did have another daughter baptised later that same year, also in Telscombe, on November 29th, called Charlotte, perhaps after James' brother John's wife.

References from the East Sussex Record Office.
Telscombe Baptisms   1813-1954   Par 491/1/2/1
Telscombe Burials   1813-1983   Par 491/1/5/1

References from the West Sussex Record Office.
Southwick Baptisms   1774-1812   Par 180/1/1/4
Southwick Baptisms   1813-1849   Par 180/1/2/1

The rear of the Manor House displaying the Saxon Tower

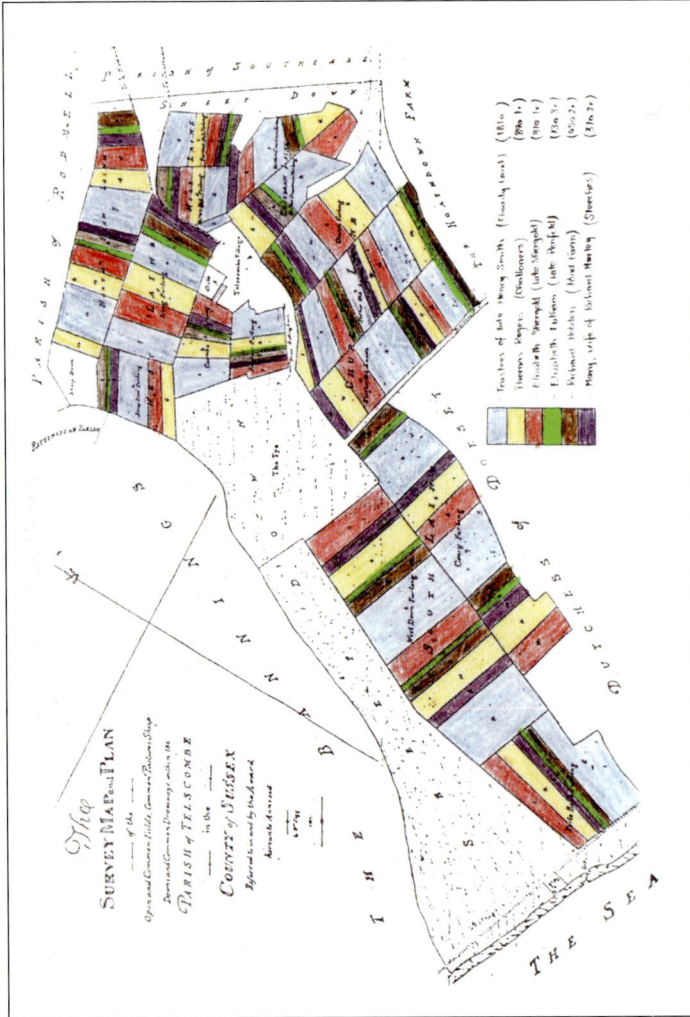

This Enclosure Award Map dated 1811 shows the distribution of the allocations of the land in Telscombe. Elizabeth's land is coloured in green. She was the 4th largest landowner (copyholder) in Telscombe Parish, holding 13 acres and 3 roods (a rood = 1/4 of an acre). From a Thesis Entitled "Telscombe c1780-c1871" by Barry N.Cornes

James Lulham = Elizabeth Hobden
Married 31st October 1804
St Laurence Church, Telscombe, Sussex

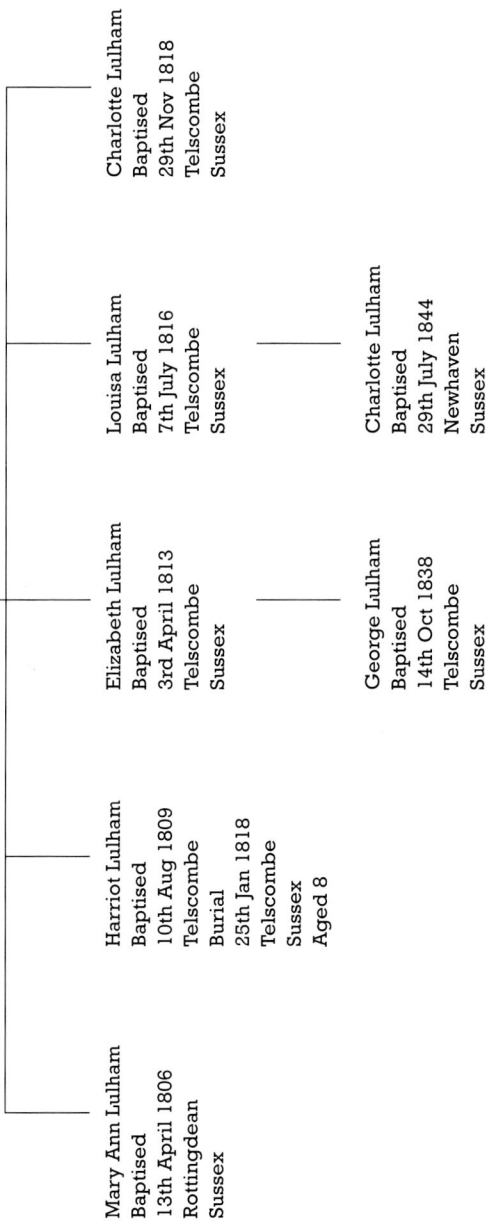

Mary Ann Lulham
Baptised
13th April 1806
Rottingdean
Sussex

Harriot Lulham
Baptised
10th Aug 1809
Telscombe
Burial
25th Jan 1818
Telscombe
Sussex
Aged 8

Elizabeth Lulham
Baptised
3rd April 1813
Telscombe
Sussex

Louisa Lulham
Baptised
7th July 1816
Telscombe
Sussex

Charlotte Lulham
Baptised
29th Nov 1818
Telscombe
Sussex

George Lulham
Baptised
14th Oct 1838
Telscombe
Sussex

Charlotte Lulham
Baptised
29th July 1844
Newhaven
Sussex

The Known children of James and Elizabeth Lulham

Chapter Three
1819

Surrey, Southwark, Middlesex, Sussex Gazette Agricultural and Commercial Advertiser.
Ref. The National Newspaper Library, Colindale
Saturday 14th August 1819

Sussex Assizes August 10th

Sheep Stealing

John and James Lulham were indicted for feloniously stealing, at Falmer, in this county, on the 24th April last, twenty four sheep, the property of Richard Verrall.
Mr Long conducted the prosecution.
It appeared in evidence, that on the morning of the day mentioned in the indictment the prosecutor, a respectful farmer, missed the sheep in question from a flock of a hundred and twenty. The next day the prisoners were found selling their plunder to a butcher a few miles distant, one passing himself as a farmer and the other as his drover.
The evidence of the prisoner's guilt being clearly made out, they were found guilty, and received sentence of death, and they were taught to expect no mercy.

It begs the question why? If they really did do it and they were both doing seemingly so well, why? They would have both known that the penalty for sheep-stealing was death. Maybe James could not manage the land he had acquired. Perhaps his business skills were lacking and money was tight. Possibly they had a personal grudge against Richard Verrall of Falmer. The present incumbent of Telscombe parish, The Revd. DA Hider has told me that folklore says that James had lost his position as yeoman and had fallen on hard times but I have been unable to prove or disprove this. From newspapers and other sources this is the story of the Lulham brothers in 1819.

After being arrested James Lulham was detained by a constable at Glynde (one report says the constable of Rotherfield). He showed "considerable pluck" according to an article in "Horsham, a millennium of facts, 949-1949 by William Albery:

"He had been confined at night in a room by the constable at Glynde who had apprehended him pending his commitment the following morning by a Magistrate. And in order that he should not escape, the constable deprived him of every article of clothing except his shirt. Lulham knew he had nothing favourable to hope for from the Magistrates, nor indeed from the Judges, and so even in this scanty attire goaded by the certainty of death or transportation if he did not free himself, he made a dash for liberty. In his semi-nude condition he got through the window and clear of the constable's house and made for his home in Uckfield,* about 8 miles away, where, he hoped, with the assistance of friend and an outfit of clothes he might be rescued from his dangerous situation. Lured by these desires, pursued by his fears, avoiding all houses and main roads as well as he could in the dark, Lulham fled in his shirt for his life. But alas, poor sheep stealer, he escaped from one constable only to fall into the hands of several others. Crossing a field at 2 o'clock in the morning, almost as it must have seemed to him within reach of his home and liberty, he fell into a trap - a trap laid not for him but for some poachers whom the constables were out that night to capture. His appearance and inability to give anything like a rational account of himself to his astonished captors, irretrievably led his footsteps in the direction of the fatal spot on Horsham Common and deprived him for ever of his hope of freedom."

*This is as stated although his home was in Telscombe (or possibly Southwick). I have checked Uckfield's baptism transcripts and there were no Lulham's baptised there between 1675 and 1829.

The Assizes had opened at Lewes on August 9th 1819. It was James 40th birthday! James and John Lulham were amongst a very large number of people to be tried at the Assizes Court.

The Sussex Weekly Advertiser;
Or, Lewes and Brighthelmston Journal.

No. 3785. Vol. LXXIII.   MONDAY, AUGUST 9. 1819.   [Price Sevenpence.]
Printed and Published at the Office of the Establishment, High-Street, Lewes.

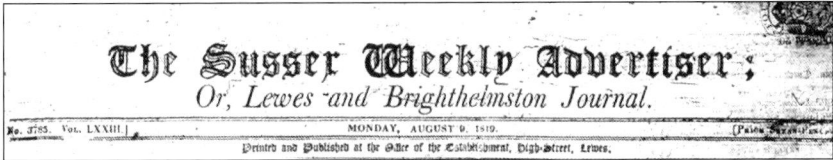

Ref. Brighton Local Studies Library

"At nine o'clock this morning business will commence in both Courts, and is likely to prove unusually heavy, there being already 31 Causes for trial, and several of them by Special Juries. The Jail Calendar is heavy beyond our remembrance at a Summer Assize, as it exhibits for trial forty-six prisoners, and many for offences of an atrocious nature, as will be seen by the following list."

These are just a few out of the long list of prisoners reported in the newspaper.

"John Piper, 42, Simon Piper, 26, charged with burglariously breaking and entering the dwelling house of Martha Humphrey, at Brighton, and stealing divers articles of wearing apparel and a Bible.

Sarah Piper, 42, charged with feloniously inciting the said John and Simon Piper burglariously to break and enter the dwelling house of Susannah and Marianne Lee at Brighton and stealing therein divers articles of plate, value eighteen pounds.

James Geer, 27, charged with feloniously killing and slaying Thomas Searle, at Storrington.

Thomas Smith, 27, charged (together with George Martin, since removed by Habeas Corpus, to bail) with a misdemeanour of stealing from the churchyard in Brighton, the dead body of Jane Heaver.

Daniel Hollis, 28, charged with conspiracy, in conjunction with others, to give information on affidavit that a certain vessel had been employed in smuggling contrary to the fact.

Edward Broadbent, 22, charged with the wilful murder of Sergeant William Watson, at Brighton.

John Lulham, charged with feloniously stealing twenty four sheep, the property of Richard Verrall.

James Lulham, 39, charged with feloniously stealing twenty four sheep, the property of Richard Verrall; he also stands charged with having escaped from the custody of William Miles, constable of the Hundred of Rotherfield.

Jeremiah Diplock, 22, charged with burglariously entering the dwelling house of Richard Verrall, in the parish of Falmer, and stealing divers articles of wearing apparel, his property, also several articles of wearing apparel, the property of Sarah Homewood and Martha Walls.

Consequently Lewes Assizes Court was to try two cases of murder and a couple of body snatchers! The majority of the other offences reported were for thefts, burglaries and forgeries. The following week the same newspaper reported of the Assizes Court that thirteen had been sentenced to death although ten were reprieved.

Sussex Weekly Advertiser;
Or, Lewes and Brighthelmston Journal.
Monday August 16th 1819
Ref. Brighton Local Studies Library

"The Assize business for this county commenced here on last Monday morning in the Crown Court before **Sir J. Adam Park,** *and in that of Nisi Prius before* **Mr Bevan Garrow.** *The Gaol Calendar was heavy beyond any precedent at a Sussex Summer General Gaol Delivery. It exhibited just fifty prisoners for trial, thirteen of whom were capitally convicted, and received sentence of Death, viz—*
John Piper, *42, and* **Simon Piper,** *26, for a burglary at Brighton. -* **Andrew Andrews,** *22, for stealing a watch and chain from the person of* **William Cook.** *-* **Eli Cousens,** *34 for stealing a gelding, at Barlavington –* **John Roser,** *23,* **John Reed,** *22,* **Mary Funnell,** *49 and* **Harriet Funnell,** *15, for a burglary at Chiddingly-* **John Lulham** *40, and* **James Lulham,** *39, for stealing 24 sheep, the property of* **Richard Verrall – George Gibson,** *24, for feloniously entering the dwelling house of* **James Luff,** *of Rusper. -* **James Cooksey,** *24, for feloniously stealing divers articles of wearing apparel, at Kirdford- and* **Edward Broadbent,** *29, a private soldier in the 90th regiment of foot, arraigned on Wednesday morning, for the wilful*

murder of **Sergeant William Watson**, of the same regiment, at Brighthelmston.

Broadbent, John Piper, and James Lulham were left for execution, the former on Friday, and the two latter on next Saturday se'nnight."

It was these three then, that were to be hanged. For the other ten the sentence was transportation to Australia for life including 15 year old Harriet Funnell. John Lulham's life was spared but his younger brother's was not. If James had not tried to escape he would probably have accompanied John to Australia. In a poster made and printed by C Hunt, Printer and Bookseller, Horsham there is also another clue as to why James Lulham was not reprieved, it states:-

"This man was a notorious offender, and his offences were more aggravated, he being situated in such circumstances that he could not plead poverty in excuse for the commission of his crimes"

So his standing in society, as a yeoman, had been a contributing factor in his sentencing. Edward Broadbent was the first to be hanged. But first I would like to fill you in more about him, his reasons for being there and the complete bungling of his execution.

Chapter Four
The Edward Broadbent Story

The trial and execution of Edward Broadbent were extremely unusual. The different newspaper reports all tell of a man who was exceedingly repentant of his sin and whose execution was the most slipshod imaginable.

Sussex Weekly Advertiser;
Or, Lewes and Brighthelmston Journal.
Monday August 16th 1819
Ref. Brighton Local Studies Library

"Broadbent on being called upon to plead to the arraignment, exclaimed in an emphatic manner, "I am guilty-but too guilty, and should be only adding more guilt to my conscience, were I to plead otherwise."
The Judge urged and entreated him to plead not guilty, observing on the fallacy of the course he had pursued, if he expected any mercy from it.

The prisoner with a woeful countenance, shook his head, persisted in his guilt, and added that he expected no mercy; his plea of guilty was therefore recorded.

Mr Justice Park however again entreated him to withdraw his plea of guilty, and plead not guilty, and requested the Common Serjeant (sic), who conducted the prosecution, to council him to that effect. He did so, and after much persuasion at length prevailed upon him to take his trial. The Jury was then charged, and the Common Serjeant having briefly stated his case for the prosecution, and examined his witnesses, six in number,………"

Surrey, Southwark, Middlesex, Sussex Gazette Agricultural and Commercial Advertiser.
The National Newspaper Library, Colindale
Saturday 14th August 1819

"It will be recollected that the prisoner, having been put under arrest by the deceased, for some act of misconduct, on the day mentioned in the indictment he was liberated to attend the evening parade in the barrack-

yard at Brighton, and that at the moment he got his liberty he levelled his loaded musket at the deceased, and shot him through the body. The deceased survived about twenty minutes, and the prisoner surrendered himself the moment the melancholy occurrence took place. The following witnesses were examined to prove the case: -

John Shannon, a private of the 90th, stated, that on the 29th June the prisoner was confined under arrest in the guard-house at the Brighton Barracks. Whilst witness was in the guard-room he saw the prisoner priming his firelock. It frequently happened, that when a soldier wanted to light his pipe, he mashed some gunpowder in the pan of his piece, to ignite some tinder; but as the prisoner did not appear to be going to smoke witness laid hold of his firelock, and asked him whether he was going to injure himself? He replied that the firelock was his own, and he was not so mad as to injure himself. Witness took the gun out of his hand, shook the powder out of the pan, and laid the piece down, at a distance of about four paces from the prisoner. The prisoner never touched the piece until a non-commissioned officer came to take him to the evening parade, when he took his firelock with him.

Examined by Mr Justice Park.-The powder must be very small to find its way through the touch-hole from the barrel of the gun into the pan, the touch-hole being very small.

Thomas Vizer, private in the 90th, stated, that the prisoner was put in confinement in the guard-house by the deceased, between eleven and one o'clock on the 29th June. Witness saw him in the guard-house, walking up and down, in a very agitated manner, flinging his hands about in a threatening and passionate manner, and heard him say-"If I go down to the evening parade this evening, it shall be worse for Serjeant Watson." John Thomas, a private of the 90th, said, he had just left his barrack-room to attend the evening parade on the 29th June, when he saw the prisoner coming out of the guard-room with his firelock; witness was standing six or seven yards from him. The deceased was standing in front of the company, with his back towards the prisoner, the latter being at the distance of about three or four yards from him. When the deceased was in the act of turning round, the prisoner raised his firelock to his shoulder and discharged it at him. The deceased dropped to the ground and exclaimed, "My God, my God! I am shot." The Serjeant Major came running out from the guard-room, and asked, "who was it?" The prisoner answered, "It was I, I am the man" and said no more, but surrendered himself into custody.

Corporal James McCabe said, that he came immediately to the spot after the gun was fired, and lifted the deceased up, he died in about twenty minutes. Witness took the prisoner into custody, and in his way to the guard-room, said to him, "Are you not a terrible man for doing such a thing as this?" The prisoner replied, "I am not, for the Serjeant was always tyrannising over me, and I was determined he should not do it any more."

Mr Isaac Silcock, the Surgeon of the regiment stated, that he was called to attend the deceased; he died in fifteen minutes after witness saw him. The bullet passed under the right shoulder blade in an oblique direction through and through the body, and in its passage went within three inches of the top of the heart. The deceased must have been standing sideways, from the direction which the ball took. There was no doubt it was the cause of his death.

When each of these witnesses were examined in chief, the prisoner, being without counsel, was asked if he would put any questions to them, but every time he shook his head in a melancholy manner, and said, "No."

Sussex Weekly Advertiser;
Or, Lewes and Brighthelmston Journal.
Monday August 16th 1819
Ref. Brighton Local Studies Library

The Learned Judge then briefly addressed the Jury, but without summing up the evidence, or making any observation upon it, which in so clear a case, he thought unnecessary. The case he said was before them and they would dispose of it according to their own consciences.

The Jury without the smallest hesitation found the prisoner Guilty, when Mr Justice Park proceeded to pronounce on him the dreadful sentence of the law, in doing which his Lordship evinced great humanity, and betrayed feelings that were tremblingly alive to the awful situation in which the wretched culprit stood before him, excited by the heinousness of his crime and the sincere penitence with which he appeared to be deeply impressed; in short the Judge was so overcome by his feelings, that he at times lost the power of utterance, and was unable to restrain his tears. His Lordship however closed the affecting scene, by urging the offender, to employ the few short hours left to him in this world in devout application to that tribunal from which alone he could expect mercy and forgiveness; and by immediately ordering the wretched man for execution on Friday morning and that his body should be given over to the surgeons for anatomization. (Sic)

The prisoner was now dreadfully agitated, and on hearing his sad fate, sunk into the arms of the gaoler and his assistant, overwhelmed with grief; at which his humane judge was so much affected, that he in consequence left the court for a short time, for the relief of his feeling, which were acute in the extreme, and did him great honour both as a man and a judge."

The Judge was very moved by Broadbent's admission of guilt and remorse. At first I did not read in the same newspaper about the execution of Edward Broadbent but instead went ahead to the following week to find out about James Lulham's hanging. But on reading this in the report I decided to go back to find out more about the Edward Broadbent Execution.

The badge of the 90th Regiment of Foot

The Sussex Weekly Advertiser;
Or Lewes and Brighthelmston Journal
Ref. Brighton Local Studies Library
Monday August 23rd 1819

"The unhappy convicts, Lulham, the sheep-stealer, and Piper, the housebreaker, are to suffer the dreadful sentence of the law, on Saturday next, at Horsham, should not the Royal mercy, in the interim, be extended to them. And it is hoped, that the executioner will be better qualified for the performance of his melancholy office, than the one through whose mismanagement poor Broadbent's suffering were so cruelly and dreadfully prolonged. See our last journal."

The Old Town Hall, Horsham

EXECUTION OF BROADBENT (Also reported verbatim in the Surrey, Southwark, Middlesex, Sussex Gazette Agricultural and Commercial Advertiser. Saturday August 21st)

(Author's note the execution was on Friday 13th August!!)

"On Friday morning, Edward Broadbent, who was on Wednesday convicted at our Assizes of the wilful murder of Serjeant Watson, of the 90th Regiment, by shooting him with a musket, at Brighton, underwent the dreadful sentence of the law at Horsham.
The unfortunate culprit left the prison at ten minutes after twelve, in a cart, accompanied by the executioner, followed by the Under Sheriff G Smith, Esq. The Rev. Mr Noise, of Rusper. (The Rev. Mr. Marshall, the Chaplain of the prison being unable to attend from indisposition) and the Officers of the Sheriff. By some misunderstanding, the Constables and Headborough of Horsham were not summoned to attend, until after the procession had begun to move. The unfortunate man held in his hand a prayer book, fixing his attention on the 51st psalm until he arrived at the

fatal tree, when the Clergyman ascended the cart, and kneeling beside the ill-fated convict, commenced his pious office by reading part of the burial service, beginning with "In the midst of life we are in death" &c. and the 51st psalm, the responses to which the unhappy man gave in a firm and audible voice, after which he repeated in like manner, the Lord's Prayer, at the conclusion of which, the executioner commenced the dreadful operations for launching the unfortunate culprit into eternity, but unfortunately he appeared not properly to understand the business, it was necessary repeatedly to admonish him, and he was told by the bystanders that the rope was certainly too long. After considerable time had elapsed, the rope was apparently adjusted, and the cap was drawn over the eyes of the culprit, and tied with a black handkerchief. The clergyman then asked him if he had any thing to promulgate, to answer to which, with the same firmness he had previously exhibited, he with classical pronunciation, uttered the following extempore prayer: -

"O' God, my Father, into Thy hands I commit my Spirit; be merciful unto me. And suffer not the work of Thy hands to die eternally. O! merciful saviour, save and receive my soul."

He then dropped his handkerchief as a signal that he was prepared. Mr Smart, the gaol keeper, ordered the man who was at the head of the horse, to move on, which he did not appear to understand, and the unfortunate man finding no attention being paid to his signal, threw himself from the cart, when, dreadful to relate, the noose being bunglingly formed, the rope slipped, and lowered the poor fellow so, that his toes rested on the ground. The gaoler now proposed to untie him, adjust the rope, and turn the sufferer off again, but one of the officers of the Sheriff called aloud for a spade, which could not be procured for some minutes, but it was at length brought, when the ground was dug from under his feet, which were held up by the executioner, during the operation, and at this period the acute sufferings of the dying man were made manifest by a DEEP GROAN.
The concourse of spectators upon the melancholy occasion was unusually small, in number not more than an hundred, consisting chiefly of boys and girls. The body after, on some account, hanging in the situation above described, more than the usual time, was cut down by the advice of one of the Sheriff's officers, and conveyed to the gaol to be delivered over to the surgeons. Two strangers on horseback, were, we understand, among the spectators, in a beastly state of intoxication, a

147 Sussex. Sum^r. 1819

Before Sir James Allan Park and Sir William Garrow } Justices &c.

3 . 6
6 . 4
Sarah Towner
Sarah Stone
John Paris

John Ellis — Burglary — at Warbling on 27 Hour 12 - D.g Ho: of Sarah Towner and Sarah Stone & Steal.g 1 Frock v 2.6 of s.d S.T. & S.S.
X

3 . 6
Pros. 6 . 4 p. John Ellis — Burglary — with Intent at Hellingly on 1st June ab.t 11. D.g Ho. of S. Baker —
X

4 . 6
Pros — 6 . 4
John Gear
Wm Kimber
Thos Hill
John Bishop
William Welfare — Thos Deacon — Geo. Weller —

James Lulham
John Lulham } Sheepstealing at Falmer on 21 April 24 Sheep p 40 of Richard Verrall
X

3 . 6 .
6 . 4 Jeremiah Diplock — Burglary at Falmer on 6 July Hour One D.g Ho of Rich.d Verrall — & Steal.g 1 Shirt v 2s 4 Hfs 4d 1 Cap v 6d of Rich.d V. 1 Petticoat v 1s Gown v 2s of Sarah Honewood & 1 Gown v 2 of Martha Walls —
X

Pros.
Sarah Honewood
Mary Welfare
Martha Walls
Thos. Parker —
Caroline Hubbard
Ann Hubbard
Geo. Ranger —
Chas Standley

2 . — . 4

ASSI 34/51 page 147
From The National Archives at Kew

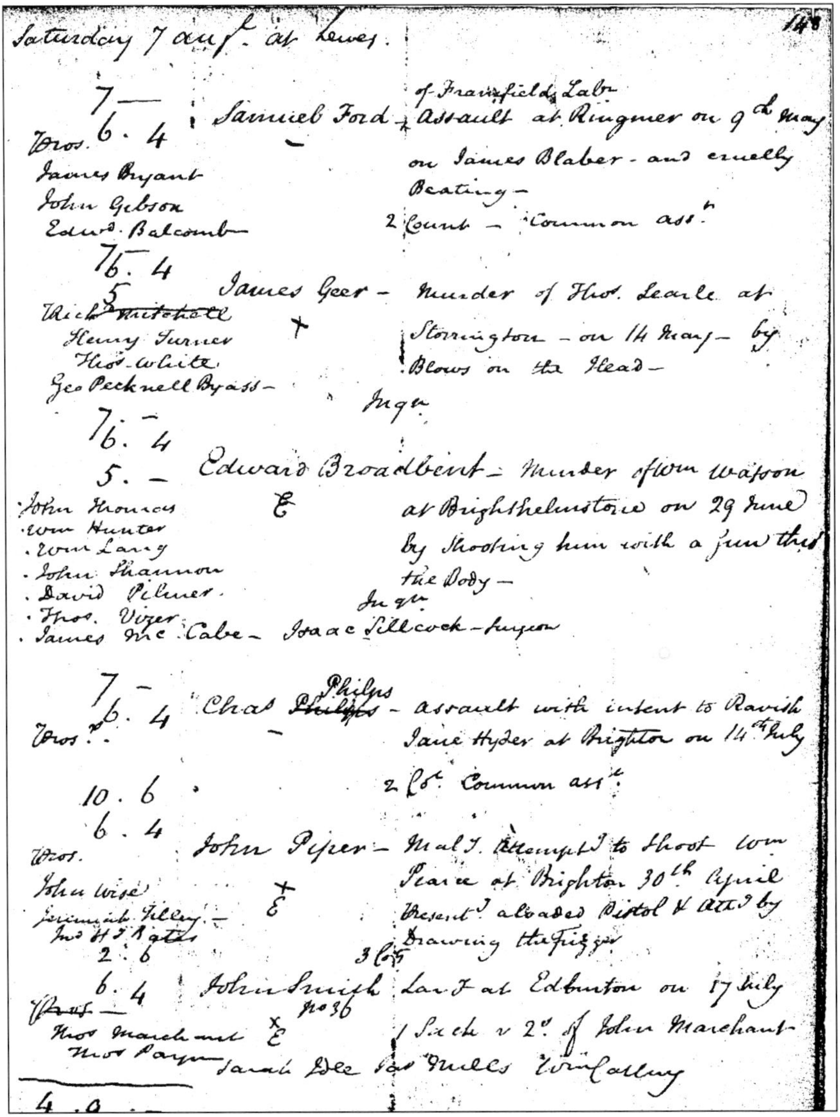
Saturday 7 Augt. at Lewes. 148

7 —
6 . 4 Samuel Ford — of Framfield Lab^r assault at Ringmer on 9th May
Pros. on James Blaber - and cruelly
James Bryant Beating -
John Gibson
Edwd. Balcomb 2 Count - Common ass^t.

7/6. 4 James Geer - Murder of Thos. Searle at
5 Storrington - on 14 May - by
Richd Mitchell + Blows on the Head -
Henry Turner
Thos. White
Geo Pecknell Byass - Inq^n.

7/6. 4
5. — Edward Broadbent - Murder of Wm Watson
John Thomas E at Brighthelmstone on 29 June
Wm Hunter by Shooting him with a Gun thro'
Wm Lang the Body -
John Shannon
David Pilmer. Inq^n.
Thos. Vizer
James Mc Cabe - Isaac Sillcock - Surgeon

7/6. 4 Chas ~~Philips~~ Philps - assault with intent to Ravish
Pros^x. Jane Hyder at Brighton on 14th July
10 . 6 2 C^t. Common ass^t.

6 . 4 John Piper - Mal^y. Attempt^d to Shoot Wm
Pros. Pearce at Brighton 30th April
John Wise + E Present^d a loaded Pistol & Att^d by
Jeremiah Tilley - Drawing the Trigger
Jno H. J. Bates
2 . 6 3 C^ts

6 . 4 John Smith No 36 Larc^y at Edburton on 17 July
~~Pros~~ - X E 1 Sack v 2^d of John Marchant
Thos Marchant
Thos Payne Sarah Dee Jas Mills Wm Calling
4 . 0 —

ASSI 34/51 page 148
From The National Archives at Kew

Instruction Books in the Assizes records show few details of the trial. The names of the witnesses, however, are shown.

circumstance, which, upon an occasion so melancholy, will be an indelible mark of disgrace upon their characters.

The unfortunate man was, we believe, a native of Manchester, where his father and other relatives now reside, and are of great respectability-he was a married man, but has left no children to bewail his ignominious end. At the early age of 16, he with a schoolfellow ran away to Liverpool, and entered on board a merchantman, which was shortly after castaway on a sand bank, from which he was rescued by a party of marines, who kept him in a state of intoxication, until they prevailed upon him to enlist, from which, however, his father bought him off-he subsequently again enlisted as a private in the 90th regiment, to which he belonged when he committed the dreadful crime for which he suffered."

This bungled hanging was to change the way hangings were to be performed at Horsham. Not in time for James Lulham and John Piper though. The following year the authorities introduced a moveable drop as used at Newgate Prison in London. The new drop was a portable wooden elevated platform, large enough for the central figure and four or five officers, erected as occasion required just outside the Gaol on the west side of the gates.

A copy of the original painting by Henry Burstow of the county jail at Horsham. X marks the spot where the new gallows were located.

Chapter Five
James meets his end

Saturday 28th August arrived. It was to be the last day James Lulham was to have upon this earth. From the reports he seems, understandably, quietly terrified. His wife, Elizabeth, was in Horsham that day. It is reported that she viewed his coffin before the hanging. I would assume that she also went to say her last good-bye. John Piper, the man to be hanged by his side was anything but quiet. He felt angry that his life was to be taken from him in what he thought was an unjustified verdict and he made sure he told the crowd of 2,000 spectators. The report states that James is 39, but his birthday had come between his arrest and his final day and from his baptism records (which also give his birth date) he was actually 40. The report:-

The Sussex Weekly Advertiser;
Or Lewes and Brighthelmston Journal
Ref. Brighton Local Studies Library
Monday August 30th 1819

"EXECUTION

Last Saturday James Lulham, aged 39, and John Piper, aged 42, capitally convicted at our late assizes, the former of sheep-stealing, and the latter of burglary, were hanged at Horsham, pursuant to their respective sentences. At half-past twelve the great gates of the gaol were thrown open, and exhibited to the view of the spectators the cart wherein the two malefactors and their executioner were seated; the melancholy procession then moved slowly on to the gallows, in the usual way, without anything particularly noticeable, except the improper sense which Piper entertained of the awful situation in which he appeared. On the arrival of the cart under the fatal tree, the Rev. Mr. Noyce, the clergyman in attendance, ascended it, and began to pray by them, requesting the unhappy men to join him; but this Piper refused to do, saying he was a murdered man, and that Pearce, (the man who took him, and to whom justice is much indebted for his resolute conduct) was perjured, that he never snapped a pistol at him, nor would he ever forgive him (here he introduced an observation which strongly marked the malignity and rancour of his heart, even in his last moments, but which we shall not repeat) he went on to observe, that there was no law for a poor man, and referred to a case at our last Assizes wherein one prisoner was condemned to death, and another, charged with a similar case, was sentenced to two months imprisonment and called down heavy vengeance on the heads of his prosecutors. The period of adjusting the halter being now arrived, he in the most hardened and daring manner, called the executioner a bungling fellow, and requested that he would not choke him before the apparatus was ready for hanging him. He was now again entreated to offer up his prayers to his offended God, but in vain, as he said their entreaties would be of no use; if they continued them for an hour, they would be of no avail. The laws of Old England he said, were fine laws, to hang a man like a dog. On the cap's being drawn over his eyes, the clergyman, shocked at his depravity, again addressed him on the horrors of his situation, and strongly urged him to employ the few minutes he had left in this world, in prayer and repentance, when he called aloud for friend John Marten, (who had been active in getting a petition signed for a commutation of punishment) but as friend Marten did not answer to this verbal summons, the wretched delinquent said, I suppose he is not here; when Mr Smart exclaimed, he is here, whereupon the culprit said I hope he will pray for me; no, said the Clergyman, you must pray for yourself; that is to myself, replied the offender, with the most indifference, praying does not consist in preaching to a multitude. He, however, expressed his thanks to friend Marten, for his endeavours to save his life; and to Mrs Smart, of the Gaol, who had occasionally tendered him good advice.

Lulham, who appeared to be an ignorant, illiterate man, died truly penitent: he fervently joined the clergyman in prayer. He had a book in his hand when he left the gaol, and scarcely took his eyes from it during the whole of the melancholy ceremony he had to undergo. He said nothing but his prayers under the gallows.

At ten minutes past one o'clock the wretched sufferers were launched into eternity in the presence of at least 2,000 spectators, who expressed but little pity or commiseration (sic) at their ignominious fate.

After hanging the usual time, their bodies were cut down, and put into coffins prepared to receive them, to be buried, as they had requested, Lulham's at Telscombe, and Piper's at Newtimber. Lulham's was of neat *manufacture, and ornamented with black furniture. His wife took a solemn view of it about two hours before he suffered.*

Soon after the culprits were turned off, Friend Marten addressed the multitude from the bar of a post chaise, on the ill consequences of mis-spending the Sabbath Day, and seemed to command general attention.

Piper, on the night previous to his execution, informed the turnkey and the clergyman that he should not take the Sacrament, nor would he for 1,000 guineas; and otherwise conducted himself in a manner not fit to be noticed. He was occasionally attended by three clergymen, but not one of them could make any moral or religious impression upon him. In short, we believe, a more hardened offender never suffered the ignominy of a gallows' although he did not appear to be wholly divested of paternal affection, having recommended his children, who are in the poor house at Brighton, the protection of Mr Rice, the governor."

What James must have gone through is impossible to imagine. Here he was, about to be hanged, and Piper next to him shouting all the time to a huge crowd. The quote from the article "Lulham, who appeared to be an ignorant, illiterate man" I consider to be incorrect. He may have seemed that way because of his sheer terror but I believe that all evidence points to the contrary.

Folklore, passed on to me by The Revd. Hider tells that James being brought back to Telscombe to be buried caused a great local scandal. It is said that many people boycotted the funeral, mostly the upper classes, the farm labourers being more sympathetic. Folklore also has it that his grave is not is the churchyard but outside in un-consecrated ground or possibly in Lewes. If this was the case then the vicar may have had some sympathy to have entered the burial in the register at all.

The Church of St Laurence, Telscombe
Possibly the final resting place of James Lulham

Lulham Close in the 20th century development of
Telscombe Cliffs is dedicated to our infamous resident

AN ACCOUNT OF

THE EXECUTION

OF

JOHN PIPER & JAMES LULHAM,

At HORSHAM, in the COUNTY of SUSSEX,

ON SATURDAY, THE 28th OF AUGUST, 1819;

WITH THEIR

Offences, behaviour after Sentence of Death,

Dying words and Extraordinary Conduct of

JOHN PIPER at the GALLOWS.

THESE two unfortunate individuals were tried and convicted at the last Sussex Assizes, held at Lewes, on the clearest evidence, on the following charges :—

JOHN PIPER, for feloniously and burglariously breaking and entering the dwelling-house of Mrs. Martha Uumphrey, situate in Black Lion-street, in the town of Brighton, in this county, and plundering the same of a great quantity of wearing apparel, a bible, and divers other articles, the property of the said Martha Humphrey. Various other indictments for numerous felonies and burglaries were preferred against him, it having been discovered that he was the perpetrator of many robberies which had been committed in the town of Brighton within the last two years.

JAMES LULHAM, for feloniously stealing and driving away from a field, in the parish of Falmer, in Sussex, 24 sheep, the property of Mr. Richard Verrall. This man also was a notorious offender, and his offences were more aggravated, he being situated in such circumstances that he could not plead poverty in excuse for the commission of his crimes.

They received sentence of Death, (with nine others at the same Assizes) and the Judge, in passing sentence on them, positively informed them that they must not expect to receive any mercy.

The conduct of the two men since their condemnation, was, widely different ; Lulham evincing a sense of the awful situation in which he stood, and attending to the serious instruction bestowed on him by his clerical attendant ; whilst, on the contrary, Piper exhibited no symptoms of repentance of his offences, but betrayed a revengeful mind against his prosecutors, and even against the clergyman who attended the gaol, and endeavoured to impress upon him the necessity of religious exercises. He paid no attention to the exhortations of the chaplain, and expressed himself in strong terms against the justice of his sentence, having imbibed the notion that his life should not be taken away unless he had actually committed murder. A few days, however, previous to his execution, he was prevailed upon to pay attention to Divine Worship, but soon returned to his former hardened behaviour.

A Sermon was preached the evening previous to their execution, but he was not at all affected.

On Saturday, about twenty minutes past twelve o'clock (their irons having previously been knocked off, and both placed in the cart) they were drawn out of the Gaol yard, attended by the executioner, to the place of execution. Lulham held in his hand a Prayer-book upon which he looked, but occasionally gazed round at the spectators. Piper could not be prevailed on to pay attention to prayer. His countenance was such as was seldom or never before witnessed, having the appearance of ferociousness, hardihood, firmness, and guilt.

Upon arriving at the fatal spot, the Reverend Chaplain descended from the chaise and got into the cart with the unhappy convicts, and entered into prayer with them. Lulham fervently repeated the Lord's Prayer, and other prayers ; and after continuing in prayer for about a quarter of an hour, the Clergyman shook hands, and bid them each an eternal farewell : the caps were drawn over their faces, and, previously to to the cart drawing from under them, Lulham was earnest in prayer, repeating, " The Lord have mercy upon my soul." and the Lord's Prayer. Piper, on the contrary, was continually expressing himself thus —" I consider myself a murdered man, ——, swore my life away ; I did not snap the pistol ; I cannot forgive my murderers : there is no law in this country for a poor man, but if he as got rich friends he will be sure to get off." While the rope was putting round his neck, he said to the Executioner " you have no cause to choak a fellow before you have half done your job ; you are a bungling fellow at it - I hope for the heaviest judgments on those who have sworn my life away ; if you mean to take my life away, don't go to putting me in much misery, mate !" and continued in this strain till the cart drew from under him. Upon being advised to pray, he answered, " a man's inward prayers are heard as well as those who pray aloud to the populace ; perhaps I have prayed more than you think for ! ! !"

" At length they were launched into " that bourne from which no traveller returns ;" and they both were, to all appearance, dead in a few minutes. Piper was observed to struggle longer than Lulham.

Their bodies having hung the usual time, were cut down and placed in their coffins, (on which they had rode from the gaol to the gallows), and given over to their friends for interment. The great bell at Horsham Church continued tolling from twelve till one o'clock, which added to the awful solemnity. A thousand persons were present.

Thus ended the fate of two unfortunate human beings, who, had they been industrious in their several callings, instead of habituating their minds to schemes of theft and plunder, might still have lived respectably, and enjoyed the good opinion of their fellowmen But vice was predominant—virtue fled : and travelling from one state of wickedness to another, they were at length overtaken in their guilt, and brought to suffer that awful penalty, which the Laws of our country justly inflict upon all incorrigible offenders. Better had it been for them had they been mindful of the solemn truth—

" The Wages of Sin is Death ! ! ! "

C. HUNT, PRINTER AND BOOKSELLER, HORSHAM.

An account of the Execution

Chapter Six
Brother John goes to the colonies

John Lulham would initially have been sent to one of the Prison Hulks either in the Thames Estuary or possibly Portsmouth to await his transportation. The conditions on these old ship hulks were appalling and often prisoners had to endure life there for a couple of years before they were actually sent to Australia. John Lulham's stay was not so long however. On July 7th 1820 he was amongst 159 male convicts that left England on board the Ship "Hebe". Interestingly, in the list of the ships prisoner passengers the name immediately below John's is that of Simon Piper, the brother of John Piper who was hanged with James. They are both listed as being sentenced to life.

The only known photograph of the convict hulks at Woolwich shortly before their removal in 1856. The hulks were established at Woolwich and at other ports in the 1770s to accommodate the burgeoning prison population. Prisoners either served their time on the hulks or waited to be transported to Botany Bay in Australia.

(Ref. HO11/3 List of convicts transported to Australia 1818-1820)
From The National Archives at Kew

It was a gruelling 153-day voyage arriving in New South Wales on December 31st 1820. One convict had died on route. The colony's population in 1820 was approximately 24,000 people and by the 1828 New South Wales census it had risen to 36,598. Conditions on board ship were fairly horrendous although it is hoped that they had improved the treatment and conditions since the first convicts sent there in the previous century.

This is an excerpt from the Sydney Cove Chronicle dated June 30th, 1790, some 30 years before and it describes the condition of prisoners arriving at New South Wales at that time:

"The landing of those who remained alive despite their misuse upon the recent voyage, could not fail to horrify those who watched.

As they came on shore these wretched people were hardly able to move hand or foot. Such as could not carry themselves upon their legs, crawled on all fours. Those, who, through their afflictions, were not able to move, were thrown over the sides of the ships; as sacks of flour would be thrown, into the smaller boats. Some expired in the boats; others as they reached the shore. Some fainted and were carried by those who fared better. More had not the opportunity even to leave their ocean prisons for as they came upon the decks, the fresh air only hastened their demise.

A sight most outrageous to our eyes were the marks of the leg irons upon the convicts, some so deep that one could nigh on see the bones."

John Lulham had arrived then, in New South Wales. I found records of him on the Internet in the Colonial Secretary's Records in the State records of New South Wales. www.records.nsw.gov.au

The first documentation of him was taken on his arrival. It was to be found in NSW 'Principal Superintendent of Convicts : Bound Indents 1820. This was more or less his registration on arrival. Details given were: -

Name	John Lulham	No.	
Court	Sussex Quarter Sessions Assized	Date	7 August 1819
Sentence	Life	Native Place	? of Sussex
Occupation	Shepherd	Height	5' 5"
Vessel	Hebe	Arrival	30 December 1820
Age	46	Complexion	Pale
Hair	Brown	Eye colour	Hazel

Condition of Leave/Ticket of Leave/Abs. Pardon: 31/631

The second documentation found relating to him was that he was on a "Nominal list of persons victualled from His Majesties Magazines, under charge of Deputy Commissary General Wemyss" dated 8th September 1821

SRNSW: CGS 901, [4/5781 p.87], Reel 6016

This list gives his name (amongst many others) that he was employed as a woodcutter and that his rations were 1½ a day. All the manual workers on the list got the same rations, servants got 1 ration and one child had a quarter ration.

On September 11th 1822 he is on a list of prisoners assigned

SRNSW: CGS 1192, [4/4570D p.72], Fiche 3290

It shows his name, the ship that brought him over (Hebe) and that he was assigned to Rev. Wm. Cowper in Sydney.

The next time John appears in the records he has been in correspondence with the Colonial Secretary's Office. The letters in the records are the requests from John and the replies to those letters. According to the description of them in the indexes they are asking for mitigation of his sentence as he is expecting the arrival of his family.

References to John Lulham are to be found in the Colonial Secretary Index (1788-1825) in the State Records of New South Wales. www.records.nsw.gov.au/indexes/colsec

State Records NSW.

1825 October 17th Expecting arrival of family. Petition for mitigation of sentence.

SRNSW: CGS 900, [4/1874 pp.134-136], Fiche 3249; 4/1874

and replies 21st October and 5th November

SRNSW: CGS 937, [4/3515 pp.466, 542], Reel 6015

SRNSW: CGS 900, [4/1874 pp.134-136], Fiche 3249
p. 134

To His Excellency Serj F Brisbane K.C.B.
Captain General and Governor in Chief
In and over His Majesty's Territory of
New South Wales and its Dependencies

The Memorial of John Lulham

Respectfully Sheweth

Unto His Excellency-Memorialist
Came to this Colony in the ship Hebey (sic) early in the year (1821) was
tried at Lewes in Sussex the year (1819) Memorialist not knowing his
sentence. Begs to say on arrival served F Gouldburn Esq. - Colonial
Secretary- and Reverend Wm Cowper chaplain since September (1822)
which he humbly trusts his conduct has been such that will merit His
Excellency's Gracious attention

Memorialist- Now hopes it will not be deemed Presumptuous in him to
approach His Excellency at this crisis Fervently haveing (sic) to be heard
with (mercy) that His Excellency's Bountiful Goodness will favour one
helpless object-that desirable liberty with that Merciful Beneficence
(sic) which dwells in His Excellency alone- that memorialist may be
better enabled to provide for himself and on the arrival of his lawful wife
and family which may be hourly expected for so great a favour
Memorialist as in
Duty Bound will ever pray

Reply

1825 October 21st Reply to the above petition.

SRNSW: CGS 937, [4/3515 pp.466, 542], Reel 6015
p 466

"John Lullam (sic)

The records of this office having been examined in consequence of your
letter of the 19th instant, I find that the term for which you have been
sentenced to this colony is "life".

By His Excellency's Command
F Gouldburn
21 October 1825"

SRNSW: CGS 900, [4/1874 pp.134-136], Fiche 3249
p.134a

John Lulham has been in my service from September 11 1822, and I have generally found him industrious and attentive to his duty

William Cowper
Sydney 24th October 1825

SRNSW: CGS 900, [4/1874 pp.134-136], Fiche 3249
p. 135

Sir
Permit the undersigned to remind your honour having addressed you a few days back could never be favoured with the knowledge of receiving it I may Bold to address His Excellency by the advice of a friend through your honours hands afraid through the Great Business it might stop your memory at the crisis I humbly trust this address will merit your Approbation to lay the same before His Excellency with your honours Benign Influence for that Great and Merciful lenity to the Desired prayer of one Individual which I venture to say rests with your honours Recommendation and with that fervency of mind always acknowledge his favour and most

Dutifully pray to posterity unborn
John Lullham

To Fr Gouldburn Esq.
Colonial Secretary

SRNSW: CGS 900, [4/1874 pp.134-136], Fiche 3249
p. 136

17th October 1825

May it please your Honer (sic) to permit
The undersigned at this crisis who came to this Colony in the ship Hebey (sic) the year (1821) who was tried at Lewis (sic) Sussex the year 1819 not knowing my sentence should wish very much to know should your honer condesend (sic) to acquaint me I would be very thankful and as you are

acquainted with my conduct Generally since my arrival most humbly craves your honer will have the Goodness of Granting or intercedeing (sic) with Commisseration (sic) on behalf of me if an humble Supplicant for Such Liberty to use my best endeavours to provide for myself Independently by honest Industry for which favour shall for ever Acknowledge the same

And ever most Greatfully (sic) pray

John Lullham

Reply 1825 November 5th Reply to the above petition.

SRNSW CGS 937, [4/3515 pp.466, 542], Reel 6015 p.542

"John Lullham

The Governor refers you to the regulations of the Colony, in reply to your late application for some remission of your sentence.

By His Excellency's Command
F Gouldburn
5th November 1825

This last, extremely brief letter, seems to imply that there was no chance of any mitigation of John's sentence. The rules of the colony did not allow it. The next time I found trace of John in New South Wales was in the 1828 census of the colony.

1828 Census for New South Wales (On the open bookshelf in the main search room of the National Archives, Kew) shows John Lulham (Listed as John Lolham), aged 58, Government Servant, ship Hebe 1820, Sentence Life, Protestant, Labourer for Thos. Cowper, Camden.(L1052)

Camden is just South West of Sydney.

His family were not listed so it seems that they may not have come after all.

SRNSW: Colonial Secretary; CGS 900, Petitions to the Governor from convicts for mitigations of sentences, 1810-26, [4/1874 p135], Fiche 3249 Reproduced with permission of the State Records NSW

In 1831 it is reported in the Sydney Gazette that John Lulham received Ticket of Leave
Ref. www.genseek.net/scons31a.htm

Tickets of Leave were issued to convicts having served about half of their sentences with good behaviour. These tickets allowed convicts to seek employment as they wished but limited their movement to a certain district for the remainder of their sentence.

Certificates of Freedom were issued to convicts on completion of their sentences or when they received a pardon. Certificates were generally given to convicts whose original sentences had been for seven to fourteen years.

Conditional Pardons required that the ex-convict never returned to the British Isles or their pardons would be void.

Absolute Pardons allowed ex-convicts to return to the British Isles if they wished. As John's original sentence was "life" a ticket of leave was about as good as he was ever going to get.

1832
John Lulham is in the NSW Convict and Burials Index 1828-1879. He is listed as buried in 1832. Ref. http:// www.genseek.net/cdeathsl.htm also to be found in NSW Convict Deaths and Burials Index 1828-1879 www.hotkey.net.au/~jwilliams4/cdeathl. I ordered the burial certificate from the Registry of Births Deaths and Marriages http://www.bdm.nsw.gov.au It cost A$24 for an online order. It duly arrived and I am afraid to say did not give a lot of information. It showed his age (incorrectly) as 46, the ship that bought him over, viz "Hebe", that he was a labourer, his abode is shown as "hospital" and that he was buried on 2nd August 1832 in the Parish of St James in the County of Cumberland, which is the central Sydney area. The cause or date of his death are not shown.

At the time of his death John had been in the colony about 11 years and only the last 4 were spent there with any sort of freedom. He may not have paid such a high price for his part in the crime as his brother James but he certainly had no easy time of it. As it seemed his family never made it there I decided to find out what happened to them. So I started my search by looking in the parish records of Botolphs in the West Sussex County Record Office at Chichester. I soon found the reason why they never joined him.

Chapter Seven
Charlotte Lulham and family in Botolphs

John and Charlotte had been living in Botolphs, a tiny parish now in West Sussex, at the time of John's arrest and conviction. They had twelve known children and a couple of gaps in the years where there may have been more baptised in other parishes. See page 50. They did not all survive however.

Stephen born 1811 was buried October 9th at Botolphs aged 21.
Philadelphia was buried March 10th 1813 aged 1 day.
James, born 1817, buried April 17th 1822.
Jabez, twin born 1818 buried September 21 1819 (Just after James and John's convictions).

Also found in Botolphs parish registers.
Jesse had children baptised there from 1834 onwards.
Harriot married Samuel Merrett there on November 23rd 1833.
John married Leah Edwards there on June 11th 1822.

The Church of St Botolphs

John Lulham
Baptised 6th Dec 1778
Falmer, Sussex
Buried 2nd August 1832
New South Wales

=

Married
18th October 1798
Rottingdean,
Sussex

Charlotte Waters

Buried 24th June 1824
Botolphs, Sussex
Aged 42

John Lulham	Jesse Lulham	William Lulham	Mary Ann Lulham	Henry Lulham	Stephen Lulham	Philadelphia Lulham	Harriot Lulham (Twin)	Benjamin Lulham (Twin)	James Lulham	Jabez Lulham (Twin)	George Lulham (Twin)
Baptised 15th Dec 1799 Rottingdean Sussex	Baptised 20th Dec 1801 Botolphs Sussex	Baptised 18th Dec 1803 Botolphs Sussex	Baptised 14th Sep 1806 Botolphs Sussex	Baptised 22nd Jan 1809 Botolphs Sussex	Baptised 20th Jan 1811 Botolphs Sussex	Baptised 8th Mar 1813 Botolphs Sussex	Baptised 11th Sep 1814 Botolphs Sussex	Baptised 11th Sep 1814 Botolphs Sussex	Baptised 6th Apr 1817 Botolphs Sussex	Baptised 18th Nov 1818 Botolphs Sussex	Baptised 18th Nov 1818 Botolphs Sussex
					Buried 9th Oct 1832 Botolphs Aged 21	Buried 10th March 1813 Botolphs Aged 1 day			Died 17th Apr 1822 Aged 5	Died 21st Sep 1819	

The most significant entry to be found in the Botolphs burial records was that of wife Charlotte. It is noted that: -

Charlotte Lulham, buried June 24th 1824 abode Brighton aged 42.

This was the year before John had pleaded for a mitigation of his sentence because he was expecting the arrival of his wife and family. Presumably at the time of his letters to the Colonial Secretary the news of his wife's death had not reached him (although it was over a year before). News travelled very slowly in those days.

It is to be wondered who brought the children up after Charlotte's death, the youngest being just over 5 years old. They may have been financially secure because in 1820 Charlotte's father, John Waters, had died leaving her a legacy of an unknown amount. I also wonder what she was doing in Brighton but I imagine that there may have been family there or conceivably she died in a hospital or hospice. I have been unable to ascertain.

1820
From the book "Sussex Schools in the 18th century" by John Caffyn.

Page 343
John Waters 1746-1820. School Master and Vestry Clerk of Waldron. (Day School/Waters School) and was also Governor of the Workhouse.
In his will dated 25th Sept 1820
Will left copyhold estate in Waldron Street and personal estate to wife Mary for life or until remarriage.
£10 to grandson John Waters (son of William deceased)
and the rest to be divided equally between
Dau. Elizabeth wife of John Pain
Dau Sarah wife of Thomas Harmer
Son Henry
Dau. Charlotte wife of John Lulham
Dau Mary widow of Charles Randell
Dau. Ann

Buried 1st December 1820

Having discovered what happened to John and his family it was now the last task in my research to find out what happened to James' wife, Elizabeth, and her family. So in a full circle we must go back to beautiful Telscombe.

West Sussex Record Office References

Some of Botolphs records for this period are included with the parish records of Bramber.

Botolphs marriages	1813-1881	<u>Par 26/1/3/1</u>
Botolphs baptisms		
(included with Bramber)	1787-1812	<u>Par 28/1/1/3</u>
Botolphs baptism transcript	1583-1843	<u>Par 26/2/1</u>

Chapter Eight
Elizabeth's Lot

Elizabeth stayed in Telscombe initially. On November 23rd 1821 she married Edward Coombes at the Parish Church of St Laurence in Telscombe Village. With Edward she was to have two more children. Sarah was baptised at Telscombe on September 15th 1822 and Caroline was baptised on October 5th 1828 also at Telscombe.

Continuing through the baptism records for Telscombe, in case there were any more children to this couple, I found the following entry: -

1838 April 3rd George Lulham baseborn son of Elizabeth Lulham baptised.

Elizabeth had been born to James and Elizabeth in 1813 and now at the age of 25 had an illegitimate son.

The Manor records show that Elizabeth surrendered her land in Telscombe to Joseph Thompsett on 24th December 1824. **(AMS. 6104 folio 38)**. What motives she had for doing this for I do not know. Maybe the sale of the land gave them much needed cash.

By the time of the 1851 national census Edward and Elizabeth were on their own in Telscombe.

Ref. Ho107/1643 folio 772

Edward Coombs, head of Household, married, aged 65, Agricultural laborer, (sic) born Portslade.
Elizabeth Coombs, wife, married, 66, born Telscombe.

The family enumerated just before them on the census was that of Thomas Pope, 33, born Rottingdean, his wife Mary, 26, born Beddingham, son Thomas, 6, also born Rottingdean, and Charlotte Lulham born Newhaven, aged 6. To ascertain whereabouts this Charlotte was to fit into the tree I looked at Newhaven's baptism records for 1844-5 and found her.

Circa 1930's

The village in the hollow

2005

1844 July 7th Charlotte baseborn daughter of Louisa Lulham baptised.

Louisa had been born to James and Elizabeth in 1816 and not to be out done by her sister had given birth to an illegitimate baby girl at the age of 28.
Sarah Coombs, the first child of Edward and Elizabeth was buried in Telscombe 1st May 1841 aged 18. Life was not really getting better for Elizabeth. She had had more than her fair share of bad luck.

I next found her on the 1861 census, using www.1837.com , but now not in Telscombe. She was to be found around 6 miles west in Kemptown, Brighton still with Edward.

Ref. RG9/592 folio 27

33 Crescent Cottages, Kemptown, The Park, Brighton

Edward Combs, Head, Married, 74, labourer, born Portslade
Elizabeth Combs, married, 75, born Telscombe.

To see if I could find a record of the deaths of Edward or Elizabeth I decided try the website www.freebmd.rootsweb.com to see if they were recorded on it (it is not yet a complete index). Luckily for me they were and Elizabeth's was shown in the quarter ending September 1867 in the Lewes area which covered many parishes around Lewes but not Kemptown. To ascertain when, where and how she died I decided to send for her death certificate.

It duly arrived and I felt extremely saddened to see that she had died in The Union Workhouse, Newhaven.
Died 27th September 1867 aged 82, in The Union Workhouse, Newhaven. Cause of death Old Age 82 years certified. Widow of Edward Combs, farm labourer. The informant was Ellen Greenwood, present at death, Union Workhouse, Newhaven.

The death certificate of Elizabeth Combs

Death Certificate - Office for National Statistics. (c)Crown copyright. Reproduced with the permission of the Controller of HMSO.

The workhouse records are kept at the East Sussex Record Office, The Maltings, Castle Precincts, Lewes and they showed that Elizabeth and Edward Cooms were admitted to the workhouse on Saturday 23rd December 1865 (Happy Christmas!) and both were described as infirm. She was buried at Telscombe. Edward had died in the workhouse on February 8th 1867, aged 81 and is also buried at Telscombe. Newhaven Union Workhouse catered for the parishes of Bishopstone, Denton, East Blatchington, Falmer, Iford, Kingston, Newhaven, Ovingdean, Piddinghoe, Rodmell, Rottingdean, Southease, South Heighton, Stanmer, Tarring Neville and Telscombe.

Elizabeth and Edward would not have had much of a life in the Workhouse. Upon entering the workhouse, paupers were stripped, bathed (under supervision), and issued with a workhouse uniform. Their own clothes would be washed and disinfected and then put into store along with any other possessions they had and only returned to them when they left the workhouse. Workhouse inmates were strictly segregated in seven classes:

CHURCH, RECTORY, AND UNION, NEWHAVEN.

Newhaven Union Workhouse is far right
Reproduced with permission of Newhaven Local
and Maritime Museum.

Newhaven Union Workhouse which has more
recently been used as a hospital.
Reproduced courtesy of Peter Higginbotham

1. Aged or infirm men.
2. Able-bodied men and youths above 13.
3. Youths and boys above 7 years old and under 13.
4. Aged or infirm women.
5. Able-bodied women and girls above 16.
6. Girls above 7 years old and under 16.
7. Children under 7 years of age.

Each class had its own area of the workhouse. Husbands, wives and children were separated as soon as they entered the workhouse and could be punished if they even tried to speak to one another. From 1847, married couples over the age of sixty could request to share a separate bedroom.

The main constituent of the workhouse diet was bread. At breakfast it was supplemented by gruel or porridge – both made from water and oatmeal (or occasionally a mixture of flour and oatmeal). Workhouse broth was usually the water used for boiling the dinner meat, perhaps with a few onions or turnips added. Tea – often without milk – was often provided for the aged or infirm at breakfast, together with a small amount of butter. Supper was usually similar to breakfast.

		Breakfast		Dinner				Supper	
		Bread. oz.	Gruel. pints.	Cooked Meat, with Vegetables. oz.	Soup. pints.	Bread. oz.	Cheese. oz.	Bread. oz.	Cheese. oz.
Sunday	Men	-	2	5	..	..	..	7	2
	Women	5	2	5	..	..	..	5	1½
Monday	Men	7	2	..	2	7	..	7	2
	Women	5	2	..	2	5	..	5	1½
				Bacon.					
Tuesday	Men	7	2	4	..	..	..	7	2
	Women	5	2	4	..	..	..	5	1¼
Wednesday	Men	7	2	..	2	7	..	7	2
	Women	5	2	..	2	5	..	5	1½
Thursday	Men	7	2	..	..	7	2	7	2
	Women	5	2	..	..	5	1½	5	1½
Friday	Men	7	2	4	..	..	..	7	2
	Women	5	2	4	..	..	..	5	1¼
Saturday	Men	7	2	..	2	7	..	7	2
	Women	5	2	..	2	5	..	5	1½

The diet of Abingdon Workhouse
Courtesy of Peter Higginbotham

The aforementioned details of workhouse life were obtained from the excellent website www.users.ox.ac.uk/~peter/workhouse and used in this publication with the kind permission of its author Peter Higginbotham.

The punishments were fairly harsh as well. Newhaven's Workhouse Offences and Punishment Book 1864-1912 (Ref. G7/27/1) show that on 3rd December 1864 Chas. Dyer was sent to Lewes Jail for 15 days for breaking ten windows. Likewise, John Pearce was sent to Lewes Jail for 10 days for refusing to sweep the dormitories (3rd Offence) on June 14th 1867.

With this sad finish I come to the end of the tale of the Lulham brothers. Their crime had caused so much suffering all around. A final twist in the tale may be shown in the Workhouse records. Elizabeth's and Edward's admission order was made by Wm. Verrall R.G.

Now I wonder if he was a descendent of Richard Verrall of Falmer who had 24 sheep stolen in 1819!

Telscombe Baptisms	1813-1954	Par 491/1/2/1
Telscombe Marriages	1813-1834	Par 491/1/3/1
Telscombe Burials	1813-1983	Par 491/1/5/1
Newhaven Baptisms	1837-1856	Par 426/1/2/2

Newhaven Union Workhouse Records.

Admission and Discharge Book	
Sept.1861-May 1867	G7/14/5
Offences and Punishment Book 1864-1912	G7/27/1
Deaths in the Workhouse 1866-1914	G7/18/2